Becoming MomStrong

BIBLE STUDY

Heidi St. John

BECOMING
MOM
STRONG

A SIX-WEEK

JOURNEY

TO DISCOVER

YOUR

GOD-GIVEN

CALLING

Bible Study

TYNDALE
MOMENTUM™

The nonfiction imprint of
Tyndale House Publishers, Inc.

Visit Tyndale online at www.tyndale.com.

Visit Tyndale Momentum online at www.tyndalemomentum.com.

Visit the author's website at www.heidistjohn.com.

TYNDALE, *Tyndale Momentum*, and Tyndale's quill logo are registered trademarks of Tyndale House Publishers, Inc. The Tyndale Momentum logo is a trademark of Tyndale House Publishers, Inc. Tyndale Momentum is the nonfiction imprint of Tyndale House Publishers, Inc., Carol Stream, Illinois.

Becoming MomStrong Bible Study: A Six-Week Journey to Discover Your God-Given Calling

Designed by Julie Chen

Edited by Stephanie Rische

Published in association with William K. Jensen Literary Agency, 119 Bampton Court, Eugene, Oregon 97404

For information about special discounts for bulk purchases, please contact Tyndale House Publishers at csresponse@tyndale.com, or call 1-800-323-9400.

ISBN 978-1-4964-2666-6

Printed in the United States of America

23   22   21   20   19   18
7   6

Contents

Introduction

Hello, moms!

I'm so happy you're joining me for this six-week companion Bible study to *Becoming MomStrong*. It's a humbling thing to be part of your parenting journey. As a mother of seven and a grandmother, my heart is with you. Moms need other moms.

Motherhood is challenging, isn't it? Anyone who has given birth or adopted a child knows what a tough job motherhood is—from diapers to diplomas. It's a 24/7, 365-day-a-year emotional, physical, and spiritual commitment. The ever-changing nature of motherhood keeps even the most seasoned of us dependent on the Lord as we adapt to cultural changes and the unique challenges each new season of mothering brings.

Mothers are always in the process of *becoming*. God uses motherhood to shape and strengthen us—it's part of the process of becoming more like Jesus. Everything God does carries Kingdom significance, and there's no better place to experience that than raising a family.

What you're doing is important, sweet mom. It may be even more important than you realize right now. The truth is that the seemingly mundane, everyday responsibilities motherhood demands can sometimes cause us to drop our swords and shields for a while and forget that we are in a spiritual battle.

Becoming MomStrong was written because my heart is on fire for this generation of mothers. I want to come alongside you, help you pick up the weapons of spiritual warfare, and remind you that what you're doing is worth it. Stay in the battle! Don't give up! Your family needs you now more than ever—and besides, good things are coming. The Bible promises that if we don't give up, we'll reap a harvest of joy (see Galatians 6:9).

Today's moms need a special kind of strength—the kind that comes from God. We need support to get us through. We need to learn how to live in right relationship with others. We need to take better care of ourselves. And most important, we need an ever-deepening desire to know God and His Word. In other words, we need to be MomStrong.

I'm convinced that God wants to use this generation of mothers to do something exceptional:

- to be strong in the Lord,

- to know who we are in Christ, and

- to impart God's strength and unchanging truth to our children.

If you're up for the challenge and you've read (or are currently reading) *Becoming MomStrong*, then this study is for you. It's a chance to dig even deeper into what the Bible has to say about raising the next generation of warriors.

Over the course of the next six weeks, we'll look at some of the characteristics that define MomStrong moms, we'll look at Scripture passages to help us understand God's heart for His children, and we'll meet some women from the Bible whose lives exemplify what it means to be MomStrong. Get ready to journal, pray, and think about how you can put what we're learning into practice in your own home and community.

Are you ready? Grab your Bible and a copy of *Becoming MomStrong*, and let's get started!

HOW TO USE THIS BIBLE STUDY

The *Becoming MomStrong Bible Study* has been designed with you in mind. Whether you want to study on your own or with a group of moms, I trust that you will be challenged and encouraged. You may want to work through the questions individually and then talk them through with a few friends or a moms' group—that's fantastic too. Build a community while you grow in your faith—it's part of becoming MomStrong!

Here's what you'll find each week:

Opening Scripture Verses: Bible passages that relate to each week's topic (If you're looking to memorize Scripture, these verses will give you a great place to start!)

Let's Become . . . : a preview of the concepts we will discuss in the week ahead

Let's Start Here: warm-up questions to help you begin thinking about the weekly topics

Let's Talk: an introduction from me

Becoming MomStrong: concepts from two chapters of the book, Scripture passages to think about, and questions to answer and discuss

A Voice from the Bible: a description of a woman from Scripture who exemplifies one of the characteristics we're talking about, plus questions to help you think through her story

Let's Review: a short conclusion to help you cement the week's lessons

Let's Take Action: journal prompts and a prayer prompt to help you apply the concepts

The study is broken down into six weeks, but the way you divide each week is up to you. All you need is a pen, a Bible, a copy of *Becoming MomStrong*, and maybe a nice cup of hot coffee.

Throughout the study, you'll find some Scripture verses printed with blanks for you to fill in. These verses are all from the New Living Translation. If you don't have this version, you can find the text online at www.newlivingtranslation.com. All other Scripture questions can be answered with any Bible translation.

TIPS FOR GROUP LEADERS

If you're leading a *Becoming MomStrong Bible Study* group, thank you! It's my prayer that this experience will be meaningful for you and for all the women in your group. Let me offer just a few suggestions before you begin:

This material can be easily adapted for a casual group of friends or a more formal moms' group, Sunday school class, or any small group of women. Sometimes large groups can hinder sharing, so I recommend keeping the group to twelve or fewer women.

Encourage the women to read the relevant chapters of *Becoming MomStrong* and complete the week's study before you meet to discuss it.

Not every concept in *Becoming MomStrong* is covered in this study. Feel free to let the conversation go where the Holy Spirit leads, remembering that the goal is to grow together in grace and truth.

If you find you don't have time to get through all the material in one meeting, choose a few specific areas to focus on. You could start with the warm-up questions and then pick one of the "Becoming MomStrong" sections to work through first, adding the second if you have time.

Emphasize confidentiality. Your group needs to be a place where moms feel safe sharing their failures as well as their successes, knowing that their words won't leave the room.

Moms in your group will likely share personal stories—and that's good! However, *Becoming MomStrong* is about more than commiserating with other moms; it's about pointing each other to God. As a leader, you can set the tone. Make sure to reserve time to read the Scripture passages and to talk about deeper questions that remind us to make God our priority.

Pray for the women in your group, and encourage them to pray for each other! Take the opportunity to build a loving community where Christian moms can support each other.

Blessings on you as you begin this journey to becoming MomStrong!

— Heidi St. John

Becoming Brave and Wise

THE ART OF TURNING TO GOD FOR WISDOM AND COURAGE

Fear of the LORD is the foundation of true wisdom.

All who obey his commandments will grow in wisdom.

⌐ PSALM 111:10

This is my command—be strong and courageous!

Do not be afraid or discouraged.

For the LORD your God is with you wherever you go.

⌐ JOSHUA 1:9

Our study this week focuses on material from chapters 1 and 3 of *Becoming MomStrong*.

Let's Become . . .

MomStrong moms know to ask God for wisdom and courage.

LET'S START HERE

What women in your life do you consider wise? Why?

What's one thing you would do differently if you had more courage?

Is fear holding you back from becoming MomStrong? If so, how?

LET'S TALK: *A Note from Heidi*

Motherhood. It's never what we think it's going to be, is it? It often requires more than we were expecting to give, but in return, it gives back more than we ever thought we could receive. Motherhood isn't for the faint of heart either—but I don't need to tell you that, do I? My guess is that you're holding this book in your hands because you see the battle you're in.

Mothers today need the wisdom of Solomon and the bravery of Esther. Sometimes that feels like a lot—because it is. The really great news here is that your kids came with an instruction manual. It's called the Word of God. For the next several weeks, we're going to dig into it together, and as we do, it's my prayer that you will feel the strong arms of God wrapped around you. Shaping the hearts and minds of the next generation is a God-sized assignment, one that God wants to partner with us to accomplish.

I'm so glad you're walking with me as we become MomStrong together. This week we're going to get started on the path to knowing God better. I challenge you to lay down your expectations right now and open your heart to what God wants to teach you. I hope you come away understanding where to turn with your deepest parenting questions (hint: not my words!) and feeling confident that you can step out in courage, knowing beyond a shadow of a doubt that the God of the Bible is trustworthy. We'll consider some sections from my book and some passages from Scripture, and then we'll talk about amazing women from the Bible who still teach us how to live MomStrong.

— HSJ

BECOMING MOMSTRONG

Wisdom

Here's the bottom line: the only way to grow in wisdom is to know God better. In chapter 1 of *Becoming MomStrong*, I write about my eye-opening encounter with Garry and Carol, who pointed me to the right place to go for parenting advice: "When it comes to parenting, there are a lot of great books out there. But MomStrong moms are looking for more than advice—we're looking for wisdom. And God tells us that the beginning of wisdom is found in knowing the Lord." How can we know the Lord? By reading His Word. That sounds simple, but for most moms, it's a battle simply to make time to read God's Word. In the rush of day-to-day life, it's easy to push our minutes with God into the "if I have time" column, isn't it?

Why do you think it's such a struggle to make time for God?

Where do you typically go to find advice for your challenges as a mom?

Why don't we usually think of the Bible as a source of parenting wisdom? How can we change that?

Since God is the source of wisdom—for parenting as well as for all other aspects of our lives—we need to seek His wise perspective as we shepherd our children. God's perspective is never temporary. It's eternal. God's desire is that we learn to look beyond the short term (our children's behavior) to the long term (our children's hearts). Consider these thoughts from chapter 1 of *Becoming MomStrong*:

The battles come in the form of everyday issues like getting your kids to put away their toys, sit still at the dinner table, and brush their teeth. These are largely just pre-war warmups, and we all approach these situations differently. But *war* is different: the stakes are higher. We're talking about the hearts and minds of our children here—their character, their compassion, their moral foundation, and their capacity to love. Matters of preference are inconsequential; matters of the heart and soul are eternal. MomStrong moms understand the difference, and while they don't ignore the battles, they know that their primary focus must be on winning the war.

What short-term battles with your children have you been tempted to focus on?

How can you focus on the big-picture war for your children's hearts and minds?

To win the long-term war of child rearing, we need to think about training our children to know Scripture, hold biblical values, discern true teaching, and develop godly character. But guess what? It's pretty hard to teach those qualities to our children if we don't possess them ourselves. We can't give our kids what we don't have. Becoming Mom-Strong means we look first at our own walk with God, asking Him to help us model a right relationship with Him for our children.

Be honest. Is there something you're trying to teach your children that you are struggling with yourself?

The comparison trap steals the joy from parenting.

What's one step you could take this week to learn more about the Bible and develop your own character?

Now before you start allowing the devil to beat you up, let's talk about something else. As long as we live on this earth, we'll hear persistent voices clamoring to fill our souls with condemnation. Weary, worn-out mothers are perfect targets for the enemy. One of Satan's favorite tactics is to use condemnation to discourage us, and he is a master at making us believe someone else could do our job better than we can. So before you start beating yourself up, remember not to allow the voice of condemnation to drown out that still, small voice of conviction.

The voice of conviction is God's voice. It lifts us up and sets our feet back on the Rock. But unless we are listening to God, condemnation can creep in and turn us into victims rather than victors. Here's the truth: every mom struggles. Of course we can't just wait until we have our lives all put together before we begin teaching our kids. They need us now—which means we get to teach them even as we're still learning ourselves.

Wisdom says, "Go deeper! Don't give up; turn to Me!" The more we go to the Word and take our questions to God in prayer, the more we'll see His guidance in our parenting struggles. God offers wisdom for worn-out moms. Aren't you glad?

What does the Bible say about wisdom? Look up these verses and fill in the blanks. (Note that these verses are taken from the New Living Translation.)

Proverbs 1:7: _____ is the foundation of true knowledge, but fools _____ wisdom and discipline.

Proverbs 4:6-7: Don't turn your back on wisdom, for she will _____ you. Love her, and she will _____ you. Getting wisdom is the wisest thing you can do! And whatever else you do, develop _____.

Ephesians 1:16-17: I pray for you constantly, asking God, the glorious Father of our Lord Jesus Christ, to give you spiritual _____ and _____ so that you might _____.

Read James 3:13-18. What characteristics does James say are not part of godly wisdom?

What does godly wisdom look like? How could the kind of wisdom described in James 3 help you in your parenting?

Look up the following verses and write down what each tells us about how we can become wise.

Colossians 1:9

James 1:5-6

When we need counsel for parenting, we can pray and go to Scripture, asking God to show us how to apply His words to our relationships with our families. What's one Scripture verse that could help you parent with more wisdom? Write it here as a reminder.

Courage

I've never met a mom who doesn't long to protect her children. We spend those first harrowing years of motherhood protecting our kids from cartwheeling off coffee tables (I actually failed at that one) and teaching them to buckle their seat belts, brush their teeth, and look both ways before crossing the street. You know, things like that. As our children get older and it's time to let them make their own choices, it's easy for fear to keep us from letting go.

In chapter 3 of *Becoming MomStrong* I write, "Motherhood is all about courage, from the moment you watch your baby take those first wobbly steps. Many of the steps they'll take after that are wobbly too. The trick is to trust the Lord as you wobble through each transition together."

What's one area where you have trouble letting go of your children and their choices?

How could you learn to trust in the Lord in that area?

If we fix our eyes on the scary world around us, focusing on all the problems we or our children might face, we'll never live with courage. We need a longer-term perspective, one that sees beyond the mistakes our children might make today, the hurt they might feel tomorrow, or the rejection they might face next month. As chapter 3 of *Becoming MomStrong* says, "God has plans for your children, just as He has plans for you. But remember, we only see the tiniest fraction of God's grand design. That's why we need God's perspective for our children—it's the only one that really matters." Our perspective is focused on the here and now; His perspective is eternal.

What struggles are your children facing right now?

How might it help to consider this challenge with a longer-term perspective? For example, how might this struggle eventually strengthen your child? How might God be using it to shape him or her?

Mothers who deal with struggles by crying out to God for courage and wisdom are doing more than acquiring these characteristics; they're also teaching their children to do the same. That's powerful! Chapter 3 of *Becoming MomStrong* says, "The reality is that we all face different kinds of giants in our lives. The question isn't whether they'll show up; it's whether we'll have the courage to load our own stones into our own slings when the time comes."

Are you facing a difficult situation right now? If so, think about the message you're sending your children about God in the midst of it. Do they see a mom who is filled with faith or fear? How could the way you are responding to this struggle reflect God's true character to your children?

How could having God's perspective help you face these challenges with courage instead of fear?

As humans, we desperately want to control what happens to us and our children. We want to avoid pain and suffering. Yet as Christians, we know that God doesn't promise us a pain-free life. Chapter 3 of *Becoming MomStrong* states,

> The Bible says that we can make our plans, but ultimately the Lord determines our steps (see Proverbs 16:9). And some of those steps can be pretty painful to take. . . . We don't always get to choose what happens to the babies we carry so carefully inside us. We can't always predict what a day will bring. But we are guaranteed this: God will never leave us or forsake us (see Hebrews 13:5). Ever.

Write out Deuteronomy 31:6 below.

How does God's presence give you courage? What helps you remember that He is with you?

Read Psalm 46. Note that these verses don't depict a calm, idealistic scene. What are some of the frightening circumstances the psalmist describes (see verses 2-3, 6)?

Why can the psalmist say that he won't be afraid in the middle of everything that's going on? What are some specific things he mentions that might give him courage (see verses 1, 5, 7, 10)?

Consider verse 10: "Be still, and know that I am God!" How can being still and understanding who God is help to give us courage?

A Voice from the Bible: Ruth

You've heard from me, but now I want you to hear from a much older woman—one who is three thousand years old, in fact (give or take a few centuries). Ruth has her own book in the Old Testament, and she exemplifies quiet courage.

If you have time, read the whole book of Ruth—it's only four chapters! If you're too busy running after a toddler, juggling five loads of laundry, and cooking dinner, I feel your pain, so allow me to summarize for you while you reheat your tea.

Ruth was a young woman from Moab, a country east of Israel that traced its ancestry to the son born to Lot and his daughter (yes, you read that right). Moab's unsavory beginning and its idol worship didn't gain it any favor in the eyes of the Israelites, who considered Moabites lower than low.

Ruth married an Israelite man whose family had moved to Moab during a famine. But in the span of a few years, Ruth's father-in-law, husband, and brother-in-law all died. When her mother-in-law, Naomi, announced that she was returning to Israel, the newly widowed Ruth was determined to come too. Her response to Naomi is one of the most beautiful passages in Scripture.

Look up Ruth 1:16-17 and fill in the blanks below.

Ruth replied, "Don't ask me to leave you and turn back. Wherever you _____, I will _____; wherever you _____, I will _____. Your _____ will be my _____, and your _____ will be my _____. Wherever you die, I will die, and there I will be buried. May the LORD punish me severely if I allow anything but death to separate us!" (Ruth 1:16-17)

Think about this: Ruth was moving away from her family, her country, her religion, and everything she'd ever known. She knew she might never return. In her new home, people would look down on her—or outright reject her—because of her nationality. By sticking with her mother-in-law, Ruth might have been giving up any opportunity to marry again and have a family of her own, because what good Israelite would marry a foreigner? Yet Ruth chose to take care of a woman who wasn't even her flesh-and-blood relation.

What does Ruth's speech tell us about her character?

What do you think gave Ruth the courage to move to Israel with Naomi?

After Ruth and Naomi moved back to Bethlehem, Ruth ended up gleaning grain in the field of a kind, wealthy landowner named Boaz. Ruth's courage caught Boaz's attention, and he had some encouraging words for her.

Look up Ruth 2:11-12 and fill in the blanks below.

[Boaz said,] "I also know about everything you have done for your mother-in-law since the death of your husband. I have heard how you left your _____ and _____ and your _____ to live here among complete strangers. May the Lord, the God of Israel, under whose _____ you have come to take refuge, reward you fully for what you have done."

Naomi eventually decided that Boaz, who was a distant relative of hers, would make an excellent husband for Ruth. She gave Ruth some advice: "Now do as I tell you—take a bath and put on perfume and dress in your nicest clothes" (Ruth 3:3). So far, so good. But then things got weird: "'Then go to the threshing floor, but don't let Boaz see you until he has finished eating and drinking. Be sure to notice where he lies down; then go and uncover his feet and lie down there. He will tell you what to do.' 'I will do everything you say,' Ruth replied" (Ruth 3:3-5).

Talk about courage. Ruth probably didn't know the Israelites' social customs or etiquette. She was already looked down on as a foreigner, and we don't have to stretch our imaginations too far to figure out that if she was seen sneaking around the male-only threshing floor at nighttime, tongues would wag, and her reputation might suffer even more. My guess is that she was terrified that night. Yet she acted.

Why do you think Ruth followed Naomi's advice?

How can trusting God and His ways enable us to act even when we are fearful of what might happen?

Ruth's story had a happy ending: she married Boaz and had a baby boy. Years later, that baby boy became the grandfather of King David. And Ruth—the despised foreigner—is listed in the genealogy of Christ in Matthew 1. Ruth was a true woman of courage.

How can Ruth's story encourage you as you consider an area of your life where you're afraid to act?

What are you afraid to lose? What might you gain by trusting God and moving forward?

Every season of motherhood offers new challenges and new chances for us to grow in wisdom and courage.

It's tempting to feel like we're in control when our kids are little. After all, we set the schedule, right? As our children grow, we still need to trust God, but the tone of our prayers changes. Things feel a little less in our control (because they are!), and we need even more wisdom. We need to trust that God will give us the right combination of grace and discipline to get to the heart of issues rather than just concentrating on external behavior.

In the teen years and beyond, the season changes yet again. There are new challenges, new fears, and new opportunities to release our children so they can pursue God's amazing plans for them. I've poured out my heart to God many times as my children have stood at the precipice of adulthood because I realize even more acutely that the trajectory-setting decisions they're making now are theirs alone. When mothers begin the season of launching their arrows into the world (see Psalm 127:4-5), an entire new kind of courage is required: the quiet kind. The kind that leans deeply into God for wisdom. We need God's wisdom to know when to speak and when to be still.

No matter what season of motherhood you're in, you've been given a choice. You get to choose to be surrendered to God. You get to choose to spend time in His Word. You get to choose to pray for your children.

As you come to the end of this week's study, ask God to open your eyes to anything you might be missing. Take time to be still before the Lord. He's waiting to give you exactly what you need for each season you're in and every struggle you face.

Let's Take Action

Did you know that God calls you friend? He does! And just like any good friend, God wants to spend time with you. Here's an opportunity to get to know Him a little more intimately. This week, reflect on what you've learned and talk about it with God. He wants to hear from you, and He wants to help you as you grow in wisdom and courage. Choose one or more of these journal prompts and write your thoughts below.

Dear God, please help me to turn to You when I need wisdom. Show me how to read and apply Your Word. Right now I need to know what to do about . . .

Dear God, teach me how to trust You and respond with courage in this situation that has me afraid . . .

God, you know I want to become wiser and more courageous. There are so many sources of advice around me, but please help me to turn to You first when I need wisdom. Teach me to trust in You and Your Word above all else. Give me the courage to act when I need to, and help me to trust that no matter what happens, You are with me, fulfilling Your good plan for me. Amen.

Becoming a Mom with a Mission

THE ART OF AUTHENTIC LIVING

I am certain that God, who began the good work

within you, will continue his work until it is finally

finished on the day when Christ Jesus returns.

⸺ PHILIPPIANS 1:6

In his grace, God has given us different gifts

for doing certain things well.

⸺ ROMANS 12:6

Let's Become . . .

MomStrong Moms are learning to find their purpose. They're discovering how to surrender to God so they can become the women He wants them to be.

LET'S START HERE

What kind of mom do you think you are becoming?

What have you surrendered in your years as a mother? Which of those sacrifices, big or small, have been the most difficult to give up?

LET'S TALK: *A Note from Heidi*

This week we'll continue to get to know God better by talking more about who He has made us to be and what He has made us to do. Nothing like jumping into the big questions, right?

I thought a lot about the title of *Becoming MomStrong* because for twenty-six years, God has been teaching me that there's a process I must go through on my way to becoming more like Jesus. God uses motherhood to give women a glimpse into His Father-heart. No one is born strong; in fact, the opposite is true—we *become* strong through years of prayer and effort. Most of us can remember the sheer amazement we felt at that first ultrasound image—the first time we felt the weight of the responsibility that comes from making decisions for another human being. From vaccines to vacations, no decision is made lightly, because each one matters. Mothers are always learning, always becoming.

We often tiptoe into motherhood unsure of the challenges every season brings with it. Each of my seven children has been part of a beautiful story that God has been writing in my life—sometimes through failure and often through tears—but always with purpose. There is always a purpose to becoming when we are part of God's tapestry of grace, part of the story He has been writing since the Garden of Eden.

Becoming is not just a step along the journey—it's the most important part. When we give ourselves permission to become, we acknowledge that we won't always get it right. Becoming requires a certain surrender. When we surrender to the process of becoming the mothers and women God has called us to be, we open the door for God to begin a pruning process in our lives.

Pruning isn't easy—in fact, sometimes it's painful. But the results are worthwhile. This pruning from the Master results in peace and righteousness.

So lean in, and let's learn together!

— HSJ

BECOMING MOMSTRONG

Becoming

Have you noticed that nothing about parenting stays the same? Whether it's a teen who seems to have shot up overnight, making his pants suddenly three inches too short, a preschooler whose vocabulary just exploded, or a baby who recently became mobile and now moves faster than a speeding bullet toward every tiny Lego piece your older kids left on the carpet, children are always changing. Their bodies grow, they gain new skills, they learn more about the world around them, and they develop a deeper understanding of God. But they're not the only ones who change. We do too.

Chapter 4 of *Becoming MomStrong* says,

Day by day, year by year, we watch our children slowly become the people God wants them to be. And in the process—through all the waiting, hoping, planning, worrying, praying, trusting, crying, and celebrating—we also become the mothers God wants us to be. In fact, motherhood is all about becoming.

Look back at your first weeks or months as a mother. What do you remember about yourself back then—your personality, your habits, your relationship with God, your ideas about parenting?

How have you changed in the years since you became a mother?

How do you think God has been working in your life through motherhood?

This changing stuff is tough. Sometimes we like the way we are. We may not be perfect, but we're comfortable with the way things are, and we'd prefer to stay right here. But isn't it good that God doesn't allow us to stay stagnant? He has better plans in mind for us—plans that require us to surrender to Him and to this process of transformation. As chapter 4 of *Becoming MomStrong* says, "It's not always easy being stretched, shaped, and twisted—even when we know the end result is going to be amazing. Sometimes the process of becoming can be downright humbling, especially where children are concerned."

Look up Philippians 1:6 and fill in the blanks below.

I am certain that God, who began the _____ within you, will _____ his work until it is finally finished on the day when _____.

How long will God be working on us? That's right—all the way until Jesus comes back! There's no getting around the process of transformation. But His work in us is good—it can change us from the inside out.

Chapter 4 of *Becoming MomStrong* recounts my story of being humiliated when my daughter splashed in a puddle she made "all by herself" in the craft store. Yep, I knew you hadn't forgotten that one. I was blown away by the grace-full response of other women in the store that day: "From that day forward, I also became much more aware of other moms around me who were in the process of becoming. The mom who brought me a week's worth of paper towels from the store bathroom said it all with one glance, as did the store manager with her lack of condemnation: grace. They understood. And now so did I."

Think of a time when you were struggling with parenting and another woman responded to you with grace. What happened? How did it feel?

I'm sure I'm not alone in having to learn humility. We moms can be tough on each other—until we have our own meltdown moments (both ours and our children's!) and realize that none of us have arrived. We're all in desperate need of grace.

Look up the following verses and write down what they tell us about how God teaches us to treat each other.

Luke 6:31

Ephesians 4:29

Colossians 3:12

Take a moment to think of a mom you know who is going through a tough time with her kids. How can you extend grace to her this week?

As we're on this journey of becoming, we need to stop every once in a while and reflect on who we're becoming. God is at work in us, and He is faithful. And yet the choices we make have a profound impact on the person we're being transformed into. Are we becoming more like Christ or less? Chapter 4 of *Becoming MomStrong* says,

> Becoming the mom God wants you to be takes time,
> experience, and grace. But it also takes one more thing:
> intention. Simply put, we become what we purpose to

become—what we're intentional about becoming. I call this kind of purposeful living holy.

Holy means "set apart." When we set ourselves apart from the rest of the world and raise our children in a way that brings honor and glory to God, that's what will be required of us: holy intention. An intention that is set apart from the ordinary view of motherhood.

What kind of woman do you think is "set apart" for God? Write some adjectives below.

What goals could you set that would help you become more holy? Consider personal habits and spiritual disciplines such as prayer and Bible reading.

Read the following passages and consider what it means to be holy or set apart for God.

Deuteronomy 14:2

1 Corinthians 1:2

1 Peter 2:9

As Christians, we are a people set apart for God. We are redeemed, and yet as we go through life, we are constantly changing, becoming something new. Let's be intentional about becoming more like Christ—becoming the women and mothers God created us to be.

Purpose

As we've discussed, every believer has been set apart by God and is becoming more like Christ. We're alike in that way. And yet every believer is also gifted with a particular passion and purpose—a unique way of serving God's Kingdom.

Chapter 5 of *Becoming MomStrong* says,

> Like me, you came into this world with a unique, God-given purpose—one that's written into your DNA. God is going to use your personality, your talents, and your natural inclinations for His glory. Yes, even your grade school report cards. Even the hard things. No—*especially* the hard things.

Do you have a sense of how you might contribute to God's Kingdom? What are some ways He has gifted you?

If you're having trouble answering those last questions, you're not alone. Being a mom, especially to young children, can overshadow everything else. But if we look at our lives with God's perspective, we'll see that the very thing we might consider an obstacle to discovering our purpose can really be a pathway. Chapter 5 of *Becoming MomStrong* puts it this way:

> I know it's easy to lose sight of our purpose in the midst of diapers and dishes. In fact, mothers often struggle to find their purpose. But make no mistake: the woman who becomes a mother will be transformed in the process, and in the midst of motherhood, her purpose and calling will be refined and renewed.

How do you think motherhood is refining you? What qualities, talents, or interests has it brought out in your life?

The thing is, mothering children during their young years is a season. If you're like me and have a twenty-year gap between your oldest and youngest children, it might be a long season. Even if your circumstances are different, it might *feel* like a long season—after all, one hour with a three-year-old can sometimes feel interminable. But looking at it from the perspective of our whole lives, it's not that long. We need to embrace the concept of seasonal living, which teaches us the beauty of surrender.

Surrendering isn't all about gritting our teeth and losing what we want either. It's about giving up something to gain something better. Chapter 5 of *Becoming MomStrong* talks about all the things I said no to when I had a houseful of small children:

As I look back, I realize those weren't just simple answers. They were a beautiful exchange. In surrendering lunch dates, book groups, and coffee runs for nap schedules, homemaking, and homeschooling, I said a resounding *yes* to investing my whole heart into motherhood. And in that surrender, I found new purpose. And in that new purpose, I found joy. . . . Part of becoming MomStrong means you may have to give up the good in order to gain something better.

What do you think it means to surrender to God in your role as a mother? What might you gain from surrendering your dreams to God?

When the apostle Paul became a follower of Christ, he gave up a lot of things he had previously considered important. Read Philippians 3:5-6 and list them.

Read Philippians 3:7-8 and fill in the blanks below.

I once thought these things were _____, but now I consider them _____ because of what Christ has done. Yes, everything else is worthless when compared with the infinite value of _____.

Why did Paul say these were no longer important? Why is knowing Christ more valuable?

Paul surrendered his old purpose to God—and God gave him a new one. Chapter 5 of *Becoming MomStrong* says,

> MomStrong moms don't surrender their dreams. They ask
> God to give them *His* dreams. They believe that as they walk
> out this life, God will walk with them. And as He does, He'll
> plant seeds for new dreams along the way—dreams that are
> equal to the season they're in. . . . What makes this kind of
> countercultural surrender possible? Faith. These moms
> know that God is doing something beyond what they can see
> right now.

What can you do this week that will help you remember that God is at work even when you can't see Him? How can this knowledge help you when you're feeling stuck or unfulfilled because of your role as a mom?

The transition from "me" to "us" can be a bumpy one.

No matter what season you're in, you are uniquely gifted by God. Your talents might be obvious (you can organize overflowing closets with one hand tied behind your back; children follow you like you're the pied piper; you can create a budget spreadsheet in the blink of an eye), or they might be more subtle (you show patience to those who are weaker or slower; you are dependable; you see ways to help without being asked). Certain things also pique your interest. No matter what your unique gifts and passions are, you can contribute to God's Kingdom in a meaningful way—in every season of your life. In His time, God will help you figure out what your gifts are, how you can put them to use, and where your passion lies.

Review the questions in chapter 5 under the section "The Passion Principle." What themes come to mind as you answer these questions? What do you think God might be calling you to do, either now or in the future? What might the next season hold for you?

A Voice from the Bible: Elizabeth

Let me introduce you to a woman who knew a lot about becoming, surrendering, and finding her purpose: Elizabeth. She shows up in just one chapter of the Bible—Luke 1—but her influence can be seen forever in the life of her son, John the Baptist.

Read Luke 1:5-7, and write down what the passage tells us about Elizabeth.

Through long years of infertility, Elizabeth had to surrender her dreams of motherhood. What dreams—about life, family, or purpose—have you had to surrender because life didn't go the way you expected?

Then one day everything changed for Elizabeth. You can read the whole story in Luke 1:5-25, 39-80, but here are the highlights. While Zechariah was serving in the Temple, an angel appeared and told him that he and Elizabeth would have a child. And this would be no ordinary child.

Read Luke 1:13-17 and fill in the blanks below.

The angel said, "Don't be afraid, Zechariah! God has heard your prayer. Your wife, Elizabeth, will give you a son, and you are to name him _____. You will have great joy and gladness, and many will _____ at his birth, for he will be _____ in the eyes of the Lord. He must never touch wine or other alcoholic drinks. He will be filled with the _____, even before his birth. And he will turn many Israelites to the Lord their God. He will be a man with the spirit and power of _____. He will _____ the people for the coming of the Lord. He will turn the hearts of the fathers to their children, and he will cause those who are _____ to accept the _____ of the _____."

When Zechariah returned home, everything the angel had told him came true. Elizabeth, an old woman by now, became pregnant! Her response to the news is lovely: "'How kind the Lord is!' she exclaimed. 'He has taken away my disgrace of having no children'" (Luke 1:25).

When the baby boy was born, he was named John, just as the angel had said. Zechariah spoke a beautiful hymn of praise (see Luke 1:68-79), and I imagine that Elizabeth was standing there with her own heart full of wonder and gratitude at the gift of this little boy. She must have felt that she had finally become the woman God had created her to be—a mother whose purpose, at least for this season of her life, was to raise this special, set-apart child.

How do you think Elizabeth's years of infertility might have helped her to grow into a woman of God? How might her struggles have prepared her to mother a special child like John?

The Bible doesn't tell us anything about what happened to Elizabeth after the birth of John. She was elderly at the time of John's birth, and we don't know how long she lived. But we can imagine that she had to surrender some dreams for her child. He came along far later in her life than she might have hoped; it must not have been easy being the only mom in town with creaky knees and white hair. John probably wasn't like the other boys in the neighborhood either; anyone described as having "the spirit and power of Elijah" (Luke 1:17) was probably an intense kid who wasn't exactly the life of the party. John didn't follow in his father's footsteps, serving in the Temple, continuing family traditions, gaining the esteem of the community, getting married, and giving Elizabeth grandchildren.

Instead he became a rather unusual figure.

Matthew 3:1-5 gives a summary of John's ministry. Fill in the blanks below.

In those days John the Baptist came to the Judean _____ and began preaching. His message was, "_____ of your sins and turn to God, for the _____ is near." The prophet Isaiah was speaking about John when he said,

"He is a voice _____ in the wilderness,

'_____ the way for the Lord's coming! Clear the road for him!'"

John's clothes were woven from coarse _____, and he wore a leather belt around his waist. For food he ate _____ and _____.

Can you imagine the conversations at family reunions? When people asked what John was up to, Elizabeth would have been left to answer, "Oh, living in the desert and eating bugs." But John was an unusual man because he had an unusual purpose: to prepare people for Christ's coming. He had a key role in God's salvation plan for all of humanity.

I'm sure Elizabeth's heart was full of love, pride, and gratitude that God had chosen her son for this very purpose, but maybe, just maybe, she longed for a life she wasn't destined to have. Maybe she wished John wasn't in the wilderness eating honey. Maybe she wanted him to be closer to her, to live a life that was less dangerous.

Like Elizabeth, we don't get to choose the life God has planned for our children. Our job is to help them become the people God created them to be. We have to wonder if John was only able to fulfill this unbelievable purpose because Elizabeth fulfilled hers: trusting God through her years of waiting, and raising John to know and follow the Lord, even through times she couldn't understand.

Can you relate to Elizabeth's surrender? How?

What do you think it was like for Elizabeth to see God working in her life and in John's life? What example do you think she set for the women around her?

What insight can Elizabeth's story give you on becoming the woman God created you to be?

Elizabeth had to surrender to God's plans over and over. Her life didn't turn out the way she expected, and yet she was filled with joy. That's because she knew she was fulfilling the purpose God had for her. And in doing so, she helped her son fulfill his.

LET'S REVIEW

My heart is on fire for this generation of mothers.

If today's cradle-rocking, carpool-driving, menu-making, tough-loving mamas could catch a glimpse of what God is doing through their efforts, I believe we would be the most passionate women on the face of the earth. Passion comes because we see something worth investing in. It flows through us when we're confident that what we're doing is anything but ordinary, and it finds a home in our hearts when we see our children in light of eternity.

Mothers are perhaps the greatest influencers in the lives of their children. That's no small thing.

As you and I stay in the fight, joyfully showing up and engaging in the battle for our families, God is going to show up too. Becoming MomStrong happens through a series of small surrenders. It happens when we say no to a good thing because our sights are set on the best things: a strong faith, a strong marriage, and a strong family.

Your family is worth the surrender. As we become the women God has created us to be, we are showing our children that we value the process of becoming.

God's guarantee for every season of our lives is sure: He will never leave us or forsake us. When we yield our plans to His, we experience His peace and His presence . . . no matter what season we are in. It's part of becoming more like Jesus.

Let's Take Action

Take some time this week to think about what we've studied, and talk to God about it. Are you content to surrender to the season of motherhood you're in right now? Do you trust Him? Here's the thing: He's at work in your life, and He wants you to join Him as you seek to become the woman He made you to be.

Choose one or more of these journal prompts and write your thoughts here.

Dear Lord, when I'm with my kids, there's no hiding my impatience, my selfishness, my lack of wisdom. I know You're working in me and I'm becoming more like You, but sometimes I get discouraged when I see how flawed I still am. And yet, when I look back at who I used to be, I see these changes . . .

Thank You for the way You have made me, with certain gifts and interests that can be used for You. Help me as I think about how I can use them in this season of motherhood . . .

Heavenly Father, thank You for working to transform me. I want to become more and more like You, but the process is often uncomfortable and discouraging. Teach me to trust what You are doing in me and in my children, even when I can't see it. Help me to enjoy the season of life I'm in, and give me the perspective to know how quickly it will pass. Guide me as I discover my passions, and show me how I can use them for Your Kingdom in each season of my life. Amen.

Becoming Free

THE ART OF LETTING GO

Make allowance for each other's faults,

and forgive anyone who offends you.

Remember, the Lord forgave you,

so you must forgive others.

— COLOSSIANS 3:13

Forgetting the past and looking forward to what lies ahead,

I press on to reach the end of the race and receive

the heavenly prize for which God,

through Christ Jesus, is calling us.

— PHILIPPIANS 3:13–14

Let's Become . . .

MomStrong moms are learning to find freedom and forgiveness. God can help us find the healing that comes from forgiving others and letting go of past hurts.

LET'S START HERE

Has anyone ever told you to "forgive and forget" when you were struggling with a hurt in your life? How did you respond?

Think about the Wizard of Oz hiding behind a curtain. In what ways does that image resonate with you? What aspects of yourself do you tend to hide from others?

LET'S TALK: *A Note from Heidi*

Writing these chapters was challenging for me. As a speaker and a Bible teacher, I want readers and audiences to be encouraged by my words. I'd rather not focus on the parts of my life that are broken. But the truth is, we all have things in our lives that Satan wants to use against us. For me, it was a childhood of secret domestic abuse. It was challenging for me to write about it—in fact, many of the pages of my original manuscript are tear stained.

Pain is part of the fallen world we live in, isn't it?

Most people I meet are surprised when they learn I've struggled with panic attacks and anxiety most of my adult life. Yet this pain hasn't been wasted, because I've seen God use my struggle to bring healing. That's what He does best, isn't it? He shows Himself strong through our weakness.

This week, as we talk about walking with God through heartache and struggle, let's turn our eyes heavenward—to Jesus, the author and finisher of our faith.

Forgiveness is part of becoming MomStrong. Forgiveness brings freedom—freedom to let go of our past and move with confidence into the future God planned for us before the foundation of this world (see Ephesians 2:10).

It's amazing what God can do with a mom who refuses to be defined by her past and instead untangles herself from the snare of offense. Jesus is saying to us, "Come to Me, and find healing."

— HSJ

BECOMING MOMSTRONG

Forgiving Others

We're jumping into the deep end here with a heavy topic. The truth is, we have all been hurt, and we all have things we need to forgive. Chapter 7 of *Becoming MomStrong* recounts the pain I experienced in my family of origin. You may relate to this all too well, or your hurts may come from a different source. But no matter the offenses, we can all get stuck in a place of bitterness, anger, and weakness if we don't learn how to move forward in forgiveness.

We need to start by being honest about our hurts. I love this quote from *The Search for Significance* by Robert McGee:

> Simply ask the Lord to give you the courage to be honest.
> Give Him permission to shine His Spirit's light on your

thoughts, feelings, and actions. You may be surprised by additional pain as you realize the extent of your wounds, but our experience of healing can only be as deep as our awareness of the need for it. This takes the power of God's light. Ask Him to turn on the light.[1]

Why is it important for us to face our hurts honestly before we try to forgive?

Who or what in your past are you struggling to forgive? Write down two or three things that God brings to your mind.

Not forgiving has significant effects on us as well as on our relationships with God and with others. Chapter 7 of *Becoming MomStrong* says,

> I didn't understand that unforgiveness was like kryptonite to my walk with God. So I stayed stuck there, a prisoner of my own unwillingness to step out of my past and allow God to heal the broken places in my heart. It would take becoming a mother to bring me to the place where I wanted to be victorious more than I wanted to be a victim.

---

1. Robert S. McGee, *The Search for Significance: Seeing Your True Worth through God's Eyes* (Nashville: Thomas Nelson, 2003), 6.

How can unforgiveness negatively affect our walk with God? How have you experienced this?

In chapter 7 of *Becoming MomStrong*, I talk about the snare of being offended. The Greek word for "offense" is *skandalon*, which literally refers to the part of an animal trap where bait is hung.

Write out Mark 11:25 to learn what Jesus says about forgiving others. In what ways are offenses like snares?

Read the following verses about our responsibility to forgive, and fill in the blanks.

Matthew 5:7: God blesses those who are _____, for they will _____ mercy.

Ephesians 4:32: Be kind to each other, _____, _____ one another, just as God through Christ has _____ you.

Colossians 3:13: Make _____ for each other's faults, and _____ anyone who offends you. Remember, the Lord forgave you, so you must _____ others.

When I finally decided to forgive my parents, God prompted me to ask Him for help. I knew I couldn't do it on my own. I needed His strength to help me lay down my anger and blame. Even when we feel the offense is too great and we're not capable of forgiving, we can trust that God's power is up to the task. Chapter 7 of *Becoming MomStrong* says,

> The ability to forgive is in the DNA of every born-again Christian. That means that when God asks us to forgive, it *is* within our power to do it. Why? Because of the indwelling power of the Holy Spirit! Our power to forgive doesn't come from within us; it comes from God.

Read Ephesians 4:31-32. The apostle Paul gives a good reason for forgiving others in these verses. What's the main reason we are called to forgive?

How can prayer change our hearts toward someone who has hurt us? How can prayer give us the desire to forgive? Has God ever softened your heart toward someone you needed to forgive?

Why does forgiving others—especially people who haven't acknowledged their wrongdoing—violate our sense of justice? How does remembering God's mercy toward us help?

As we deal with hurts from our past, we need to look carefully at how we're modeling forgiveness for our own children. If you're struggling to forgive a friend, a parent, or a coworker, it's helpful to remember that God has modeled forgiveness by forgiving us. He's not just commanded us to forgive others; He's lived out what forgiveness looks like.

We might not have had great examples in our own family of origin, but that doesn't mean we're stuck passing on the same failures to our children. Chapter 7 of *Becoming MomStrong* says,

> Part of our job as mothers is to equip our kids to handle
> things better than we did, even as we're in the process
> of learning ourselves. . . . MomStrong moms model
> forgiveness for their children not only because God requires

it but also because they want our children to be pure of
heart, obedient to God, and strong for battle.

Letting Go of Your Past

Chapter 8 of *Becoming MomStrong* tells the story of my Bible college professor,
Dr. Mitchell, who shared these profound words in a lecture: "Before God
will use you greatly, He will wound you deeply. Are you ready to be pruned
by the Master?". Our reaction to the idea of God pruning us will vary
widely depending on how much we trust God. Do you feel like He causes
pain for no reason? Or do you see Him as a master gardener who knows
what He's doing and has the best plans in mind for us?

What comes to mind when you imagine God "pruning" you? How can you increase your trust in His process and His heart?

How might it make a difference to think of the challenges in your past as God's "pruning"? What do you think the end goal of His pruning might be in your life?

Look back over the past few years of your life and identify one or two ways that God has pruned you. How do you see that pruning bearing fruit in your children's lives? How has God used that pruning to change patterns from those of your family of origin?

Chapter 8 of *Becoming MomStrong* describes part of my process of learning where God is in the midst of our pain:

> The Bible says that *everything* works together for good for those who are called according to His purpose. *In other words*:

if God allows it, it's for a purpose. And though it may hurt like nobody's business, nothing can change the truth of God's promises to us or His heart toward us. His heart is good; His purposes are good. Realizing this challenged and eventually changed my perspective on the purpose of suffering.

Write out Romans 8:28 below. What does this verse say about suffering?

Look back on a past struggle you've had in parenting. How have you seen God bring good out of the struggle, even though it was difficult?

Don't let something from your past keep you from the future God has for you.

In chapter 8 of *Becoming MomStrong*, I reflect on the unexpectedly redemptive nature of the pain I experienced:

> Looking back, I realize that the grief I walked through . . . was a gift. According to God, my pain wasn't without meaning. The *truth*, as it turned out, was just as God promised in Romans 8:28. He wanted to use it for His glory. My story, His glory. Ever true to His Word, God didn't waste my tears, and He won't waste yours. If you're struggling with past pain, precious mom, take it to the One who is acquainted with grief. . . . Rather than let your past determine your future,

rather than allow your pain to determine your present, allow God to use these things for good. God will use your pain for His purposes in beautiful ways that will bring beauty from ashes as you trust Him. I promise.

Read Isaiah 61:3 and fill in the blanks below.

To all who mourn in Israel, he will give a crown of _____ for ashes, a joyous _____ instead of mourning, festive _____ instead of despair.

What does this verse tell us about God's ability to bring good out of suffering?

In many cases, our past is what shapes us and causes us the most suffering. Chapter 8 of *Becoming MomStrong* tells about the negative messages I heard from my father that made me feel like I would never measure up. I hid my true self from most people around me, sure that they would no longer like me if they saw how weak I really was. My struggle came to a head when I was pregnant with my first daughter, terrified that my father was right in saying that I would be an awful mother. When I finally expressed this fear to our birth instructor, she shared some beautiful words with me: "Don't you know who you are? You are new! God has made you new! You are a new creation, and your baby is the beginning of the healing that is coming, if you'll let God shine His love into the deep places in your heart. You. Are. New. Do you believe that?"

Are you carrying the burden of negative or wrong thinking from your past into your present?

In what areas do you need to know that you are made new—that you are not bound to your past?

Read 2 Corinthians 5:17 and fill in the blanks below.

Anyone who belongs to _____ has become a _____ person. The old life is _____; a new life has _____!

God has made us new! Yet sometimes we feel stuck in what has come before. In chapter 8 of *Becoming MomStrong*, I write

> Many of our struggles as mothers are rooted in the past. Some of us grew up in circumstances that made us feel vulnerable and afraid, so we struggle with the need to control everything around us in an attempt to feel protected. Some of us were bullied as children, and we struggle with self-hatred. Others battle constant fear and anxiety. We all have something that brings us to the end of ourselves.

Regardless of our unique circumstances, when we peel back the layers of self-protection, we quickly discover that we are all in need of a Savior. MomStrong moms are okay with needing help because they know it's not a bad thing to be weak. After all, weakness is where we discover how strong God is. It's where His strength is found.

Healing can never be found apart from the truth.

Read 2 Corinthians 12:7-10, one of the most famous Bible passages about weakness. What does Paul say was the purpose of his "thorn in the flesh"?

Why do you think God's power works best in weakness? What does this truth tell us about God?

What words in verses 9-10 show us Paul's changed attitude toward his weakness? How is it possible for us to take pleasure in our weaknesses or sufferings?

In our culture, weakness is something we tend to camouflage. We're like the old man pretending to be the Wizard of Oz, hiding behind a curtain, terrified that someone will see the real him. But God has set us free! He is not ashamed of our weaknesses. He tells us to boast in them because they ultimately show off His power.

God uses our weaknesses to change us and sanctify us. As chapter 8 of *Becoming MomStrong* states,

> If you're a woman living in fear behind a curtain, I challenge you to step out from behind it. Look your fears and weakness in the face, and declare these truths with me. You are new! You were born to be free, born to know the One who desires to be a "lamp unto [your] feet and a light unto [your] path" (Psalm 119:105, KJV). God is in the business of restoring broken people—of making the blind see, the lame walk, and the weak strong (see Matthew 11:5)—and He is rewriting your story the same way He is rewriting mine.

What do you tend to hide behind—your appearance, your busyness, your online persona? What parts of your facade are you longing to lay down?

Identify one person in your life who might be a safe person to confide in, and ask if you can meet with her. It's okay to start small! Decide on one thing you want this person to know, and then take a step toward sharing the authentic you.

A Voice from the Bible: Rahab

This week we're looking at a woman of the Old Testament who let go of her past like few others: Rahab.

Rahab's story is found in Joshua 2 and 6. Let's set the scene: the Israelites had escaped from Egypt more than forty years earlier, thanks to God's miraculous rescue at the Red Sea. But they had been wandering in the wilderness for a generation because the people didn't trust the Lord. When it was finally time for the people of God to move into the Promised Land, one of the first obstacles was the walled city of Jericho.

One of the Israelite leaders, Joshua, sent two spies ahead to scope out the city and the surrounding land. They stayed at the house of a woman named Rahab. She is called an innkeeper in some Scripture translations but is more often referred to as a prostitute. This woman had a past with a capital *P*. The Israelites had been warned about women like her.

Somehow the king found out that two Israelite spies had arrived in his city and were staying with Rahab. He ordered her to produce the men—and that's when she did something surprising.

Read Joshua 2:2-7. What did Rahab say to the king's messengers? What had she really done with the men?

We're used to reading Bible stories knowing that the Israelites are the good guys, so we might think it makes perfect sense for Rahab to be on their side. But consider the situation from her perspective. She had grown up in Jericho, and now she was essentially committing treason. If anyone found out she had hidden the spies, she would be done for. Why would she take such a risk?

Read Joshua 2:8-13 and fill in the blanks below.

Before the spies went to sleep that night, Rahab went up on the roof to talk with them. "I know the LORD has given you this _____," she told them. "We are all afraid of you. Everyone in the land is living in terror. For we have heard how the LORD made a dry path for you through the _____ when you left Egypt. . . . No one has the courage to fight after hearing such things. For the LORD your God is the _____ of the heavens above and the earth below. Now swear to me by the _____ that you will be kind to me and my family since I have helped you. Give me some guarantee that when Jericho is conquered, you will let me live, along with my father and mother, my brothers and sisters, and all their families."

What motivated Rahab to help the spies? What did she want in return?

Rahab was banking her life—and the lives of her family members—on the fact that God is real and powerful. She wasn't the only one who had heard the stories about how God had delivered the Israelites, but she was the only one who acted on what she'd heard. She believed and she acted, even though it cost her a home, a culture, and a whole way of life.

You know the story: the Israelites marched around Jericho for seven days, and on the seventh day the walls fell. But Rahab and her family were saved. Joshua 6:25 tells her happy ending: "She lives among the Israelites to this day."

Scripture says that foreigners were to be welcomed into the community as long as they followed the Israelite laws (see Leviticus 20:2, for example). That means that to stay with the Israelites, Rahab and her family had to agree to abide by the Mosaic law. No more idols. No more pagan rituals or sacrifices. No more prostitution. Instead, they followed the Israelite customs and were now considered equal followers of the one true God.

The Bible mentions Rahab a few more times. Look up the following verses and write down what they tell us about her.

Matthew 1:5

Hebrews 11:31

James 2:25

Rahab went on to become an ancestor of King David (and thus Jesus). She's mentioned in the Hebrews 11 "hall of faith" and is cited by James as an example of faith. That's a pretty dramatic change from a woman most of us wouldn't have chosen as a role model for our daughters. This woman was not defined by her past. She knew she was changed, new, and accepted as a child of God.

I bet there were times when voices from Rahab's past threatened to hurt her: *You don't belong with these people. God doesn't really love you. You're not good enough.* But Rahab knew she didn't have to listen, because God had changed her. She wasn't the same person anymore. She wasn't defined by her past—and neither are you.

How can Rahab's example encourage you as you try to let go of your past and move forward in freedom?

Read Philippians 3:13-14. What does this passage tell us to strive toward?

The world's definition of forgiveness stands in sharp contrast to the kind of forgiveness we learn about in the Bible. The world says that forgiveness is optional; God says it's an act of obedience. The world says that forgiveness is something you extend if you feel like it—and only after the offender asks for it. Romans 5:8 shows us what Christ-honoring forgiveness looks like: "God shows his love for us in that while we were yet sinners Christ died for us" (RSV). Paul goes on to say that "while we were enemies we were reconciled to God by the death of his Son, much more, now that we are reconciled, shall we be saved by his life" (Romans 5:10, RSV).

When God allowed His beloved, sinless Son to die in our place, He set the bar for forgiveness of those who have wronged us. While we were still shaking our fist at God, unwilling to acknowledge our own sin, God sent Jesus to die so that we might live. That's what true love does. It forgives. If we're going to raise a generation of children who can walk in freedom, we must first show them what forgiveness looks like. Praise God! Through the power of the Holy Spirit, we can forgive others.

Let's Take Action

Take some time this week to write out your thoughts to God. Choose one or more of these journal prompts.

Dear God, You know I'm having a hard time letting go of some past hurts. It seems impossible, but I know You've made it possible through Your Holy Spirit. Please help me forgive . . .

Dear God, so often I try to hide because I don't want others to see my weaknesses. Teach me that You can work through my weaknesses. Show me how I can be more honest about who I am . . .

Lord God, I'm grateful that You don't allow my pain to be wasted. Instead, You use it for my good. Help me to trust that You are doing a good work in me. Help me to believe that I'm not defined by my past. Rather, I'm defined by You and the new work You're doing in my life. Amen.

Becoming Emotionally Strong

THE ART OF LIVING IN COMMUNITY

The lips of the godly speak helpful words.

— PROVERBS 10:32

LORD, you know the hopes of the helpless.

Surely you will hear their cries and comfort them.

— PSALM 10:17

Our study this week focuses on material from chapters 9 and 10 of *Becoming MomStrong*.

Let's Become . . .

MomStrong moms are learning to become drama-free. We can avoid drama and find help in our grief when we pursue the peace and hope that come from God.

LET'S START HERE

How would you define *drama*?

Where does drama show up in your life? How do you find yourself being drawn into it?

Where do you turn when you feel grieved over broken relationships or difficult circumstances?

In what unhealthy ways do you tend to deal with hurt? What brings you comfort and hope when you're suffering?

LET'S TALK: *A Note from Heidi*

Drama. You have yours; I have mine. But I've decided that *d* is for *drama*, and it comes from the devil! (See how I did that?) This week we're going to talk about why it's important to "just say no" to drama and how we can become drama-free mamas! Doesn't that sound amazing?

Sometimes conflict is avoidable (drama), and sometimes it's not (opportunity). Regardless of where you are in your relationships, God wants to teach you to be a better reflection of His heart for others. God cares about our friendships, our marriages, and our families.

A few wonderful things happen when we follow God's relationship rules. The first wonderful by-product of becoming drama-free is that we find peace. When peace reigns in our hearts, we are more able to listen for the still, small voice of the Holy Spirit, and we're better equipped to handle the inevitable struggles that each of us will encounter on our journey to becoming MomStrong.

— HSJ

BECOMING MOMSTRONG

Avoiding Drama

You may never have "vague-booked" about an offense like I did (see chapter 9 of *Becoming MomStrong*), but I bet you've had some of your own failures in handling confrontation. Sometimes they stem from our good old sinful nature, but other times they happen because we've never seen a better way modeled. Chapter 9 of *Becoming MomStrong* says,

I believe we can handle our conflict more wisely—and set our children on a path to handling their own strife better than we have. There are no guarantees, of course, but emotionally healthy moms have a much better chance of instilling emotional health into their own children, too. It all starts at home.

What are some positive and negative ways your children handle conflict?

Positive ways of handling conflict	Negative ways of handling conflict

The truth is, some of us are so used to getting caught up in drama that it starts to feel normal, and we even enjoy it. Are you a drama addict? Review the telltale signs from chapter 9 of *Becoming MomStrong*. Do you

- insert yourself into situations where your presence isn't necessary or wanted?

- get people stirred up over things that are of little to no significance?

- "need" to know about relationships that aren't your own?

- live in the past?

- believe or claim that your motives for stirring up drama are pure (e.g., "I just want to help!")?

How would your life change if you made a bigger effort to avoid unnecessary drama?

Drama is all around us, but we don't have to be a part of it. It drains us of emotional energy, has the potential to wreck relationships, and is not pleasing to God. He wants us to use our words wisely.

The book of Proverbs has a lot to say about our words—and much of it is very blunt. Look up the following Scripture passages about our words and fill in the blanks below.

Proverbs 18:21: The tongue can bring _____ or _____; those who love to talk will reap the _____.

Proverbs 15:1: A _____ answer deflects _____, but _____ words make tempers _____.

Proverbs 25:23: As surely as a north wind brings _____, so a _____ tongue causes _____!

Proverbs 16:24: _____ words are like honey—sweet to the _____ and healthy for the _____.

Proverbs 12:18-19: Some people make cutting remarks, but the words of the _____ bring _____. _____ words stand the test of time, but lies are soon _____.

Fortunately God doesn't just command us to guard our tongues; He also promises to help us do so. Chapter 9 of *Becoming MomStrong* says,

You may not feel like you have the inner strength to avoid drama, but take heart—you don't have to do this alone. When we listen for the Holy Spirit, He will guide our words and our actions. We can learn to live in such a way that we sense God's hand on our shoulders (or in my case, over my mouth!) whenever we're tempted to stir up or engage in drama. When we walk with the Spirit, He tells us when to speak up and when to be quiet. He's good like that. So when you sense God saying, *This isn't for you,* quietly excuse yourself.

Think of a situation where you often hear gossip or drama. Maybe it's in the break room at work, in the school pickup line, or even in the church foyer. (Sad but true, right?) How could you disengage yourself from the drama in a way that pleases God? What could be your trigger to walk away?

In Matthew 18:15-17, Jesus lays out some basic steps for us to follow when someone else has sinned against us. First, we're to go to the person privately and try to resolve the situation. If that doesn't work, we should go back with two or three others who can help mediate the conflict. If that still doesn't work, we're to take the problem to the church. While this approach is specifically intended for believers, the concept of going directly to the person we have a problem with is wise advice for our interactions with anyone. Yes, this is hard. It's easier to talk about what someone did than it is to approach them directly with our hurt. But Jesus' way leads away from division and toward peace.

When have you been tempted to talk about someone who hurt you rather than going to him or her directly?

Why is it so hard to approach someone directly to resolve a problem?

Why do you think Jesus took the time to teach us how to handle conflict?

As believers, we are called to unity and peace. Chapter 9 of *Becoming MomStrong* says, "In Ephesians 4:3, Paul instructs the church to 'make every effort to keep yourselves united in the Spirit, binding yourselves together with peace.' God cares about His children living in right relationship with Him and with each other."

Review the five tips in chapter 9 for staying drama-free (listen; don't drag others into the mud; stop trespassing; stop, drop, and roll; don't stir things up). Which of these tips is most helpful to you as you try to change the way you talk to and about others? How can you put one of these strategies into practice this week?

Finding Hope in Grief

If our experiences with drama teach us anything, it's that people can be mean and thoughtless—ourselves included! With so many hurting people walking around, it's no surprise that we hurt each other. A lot. We experience grief because of rejection and broken relationships, because of illness and loss, and because of our own self-focus. And our children will hurt too. We can't change that, but we do have control over the way we deal with it.

Chapter 10 of *Becoming MomStrong* says,

> No matter how much we try to protect them, at some point our kids are going to face rejection. When we face it ourselves, it can be an opportunity to teach our children healthy ways to handle the emotions that follow. MomStrong moms trust God to help them model healing for their children—even if it means your kids see you cry.

What sorrows have your children observed in your life?

It's time to say no to drama, mama!

What do you think they have learned about faith from watching you experience grief?

What would you like your children to learn from the way you respond to sadness?

Chapter 9 of *Becoming MomStrong* says,

> God doesn't expect us to be happy all the time. He understands that we aren't always in a hallelujah place in our lives. He loves us and accepts us right where we are. And what's more, the Bible teaches that He's actually *closer* to us when we're struggling and suffering than at any other time in life.

Read the following Scripture verses. What do they tell us about God's response to us when we hurt?

Psalm 34:18

Psalm 23:4

Psalm 10:17

Matthew 5:4

In chapter 10 of *Becoming MomStrong*, I talk about Jesus' humanity and His example in suffering:

> Of all the characteristics I love about my God, the one that touches me most is that He has made me in His image. If we are emotional beings, we'd better believe that God is also emotional. God grieves too. He isn't aloof, indifferent, or unaware when His children are grieving. Instead, He is present in our suffering. He understands it because He, too, has suffered.

Read Mark 14:46-50. The disciples were with Jesus in the garden of Gethsemane when armed men came to arrest Him. What did the disciples do?

Jesus was about to experience the terrible physical pain of the Crucifixion and the spiritual pain of being separated from God. On top of that, He felt the emotional pain of being deserted by His closest friends and followers. He understands our deepest loneliness and isolation because He was more alone than we'll ever have to be.

Chapter 10 of *Becoming MomStrong* says,

> God doesn't leave us alone in our grief. In a beautiful exchange, Jesus offers His grace for our sorrows, His peace for our pain, and His hope for our fears. There's grace in abundance for the brokenhearted mom at the feet of Jesus Christ. He offers healing from the past and hope for the future. It's all there—we need only ask.

Read Romans 5:3-5 and fill in the blanks below.

We can _____, too, when we run into problems and trials, for we know that they help us develop _____. And endurance develops strength of _____, and character strengthens our confident _____ of salvation. And this hope will not lead to _____. For we know how dearly God loves us, because he has given us the Holy Spirit to fill our hearts with his love.

The days go by
so slowly, yet
the years go by
so fast.

Why doesn't our hope of salvation disappoint us? What is it rooted in?

When our hope is rooted in God Himself—who He is and what He has done—then we can never lose it. His goodness will never change. His work of salvation will never fade away. Our hope in Him is solid and tangible, a worthwhile anchor for our lives.

Although lessons in grief and suffering never come easily, they always carry purpose. When we learn to have hope in our own grief and sorrow, we're better able to help others who are struggling. In chapter 10 of *Becoming MomStrong*, I write about my experience after my miscarriage:

> I learned a couple of painful lessons from the loss of our baby—chief among them that I don't ever want to be in a hurry to fix someone else's pain. It's difficult to know what to say when someone is grieving, and we often try to fill the empty space with words. The words are meant to bring a positive out of a negative, but in reality, all they do is downplay the legitimate pain that person is experiencing. In reality, the person who is suffering doesn't need our words. They just need our presence.

We've all had people say unhelpful things to us when we're hurting. When have people responded well to you in the midst of grief? What was comforting to you? How might you respond to others who are hurting, including your own children?

Read 2 Corinthians 1:3-4. How are we equipped to comfort others?

In the midst of all the hurt in this world, we can rest in God's promise of hope, as I write in chapter 10 of *Becoming MomStrong*:

> Our hope is this: one day God is going to settle the score. One day God will wipe away every tear from our eyes. One day God will make all things new. When I read my Bible, I am reminded that this life isn't all there is! Hallelujah! Our hope is found in Jesus, and because of Him, we have a wonderful eternity to look forward to: "No eye has seen, no ear has heard, and no mind has imagined what God has prepared for those who love him" (1 Corinthians 2:9).

List some reasons for our hope. How does this rock-solid hope change the way we approach our struggles?

A Voice from the Bible: Hagar

Our story for this week features one of the most famous couples in all of Scripture: Abraham and Sarah. And yet the star of our story is neither the patriarch nor his wife. It's the servant girl—a young Egyptian woman named Hagar who found hope in God in the midst of a whole lot of drama. You can read her story in Genesis 16 and 21.

There's no sugarcoating the messiness in this story. When we read it, we come face-to-face with some details of ancient culture that frankly don't seem to make a lot of sense, plus plain old sinful behavior from people who should have known better. And yet God is present.

You may know the basic outline of this story: God had promised Abraham that he would have a son—in fact, He had promised Abraham that he'd have so many descendants they couldn't even be counted. (Quick note for the sake of accuracy: Abraham's name was Abram at this point of the story, and Sarah was Sarai. God changed their names later. But we'll keep it simple here and just call them Abraham and Sarah.) Abraham believed that promise, yet the years kept going by. Abraham and Sarah weren't getting any younger. So Sarah came up with her own idea.

Read Genesis 16:1-3. Anyone feel like Sarah's plan might be a bad idea? Yep. Not only did it go against God's directions, but it also opened up a huge can of worms for these two women. Having a servant bear children for her mistress was a common practice in some ancient cultures as a way to deal with infertility. Think of it as a kind of surrogacy, albeit one where the surrogate mother probably had little choice in the matter. Servants were often thought of as property, so I'm guessing no one asked Hagar how she felt about this little arrangement. Given all that baggage, it's no surprise that things quickly went south. Hagar became pregnant, and Scripture says that "she began to treat her mistress, Sarai, with contempt" (Genesis 16:4). Sarah got angry and treated Hagar so badly that she ran away.

Both Hagar and Sarah ratcheted up the drama in this situation. Why do you think Hagar reacted the way she did to her pregnancy? Why might Sarah have been angry?

Here's where God enters the picture. Read Genesis 16:7-13 and fill in the blanks below.

The angel of the LORD found Hagar beside a spring of water in the wilderness, along the road to Shur. The angel said to her, "Hagar, Sarai's servant, where have you come from, and where are you going?"

"I'm _____ from my mistress, Sarai," she replied.

The angel of the LORD said to her, "_____ to your mistress, and submit to her authority." Then he added, "I will give you more _____ than you can count."

And the angel also said, "You are now pregnant and will give birth to a _____. You are to name him Ishmael (which means "_____"), for the LORD has heard your cry of distress." . . .

Thereafter, Hagar used another name to refer to the LORD, who had spoken to her. She said, "You are the God who _____."

What two descriptions of God are used in verses 11 and 13?

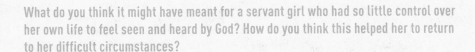

What do you think it might have meant for a servant girl who had so little control over her own life to feel seen and heard by God? How do you think this helped her to return to her difficult circumstances?

When have you felt seen and heard by God? How did this encourage you in your circumstances?

Hagar went back to Sarah and Abraham. She eventually had a son and named him Ishmael, just as the angel had told her. All was good for several years, with Ishmael living a charmed life as Abraham's heir. But when Sarah became pregnant and gave birth to a son, Isaac, who was clearly the son of God's promise, things began to change for Hagar. Where did this leave Ishmael?

Ishmael's birth had been Sarah's idea, and yet when Isaac started growing up, she began to see Ishmael as a threat to her son's inheritance. She demanded that Abraham send him away. (Let's be honest: Sarah comes out looking pretty bad in this story.) Hagar and Ishmael were left wandering in the desert, where they eventually ran out of water. The situation looked desperate.

Read Genesis 21:17-19 and fill in the blanks below.

God heard the boy crying, and the angel of God called to Hagar from heaven, "Hagar, what's wrong? Do not be _____! God has _____the boy crying as he lies there. Go to him and comfort him, for I will make a great _____ from his descendants."

Then God opened Hagar's eyes, and she saw a _____ full of water. She quickly filled her water container and gave the boy a drink.

How did this encounter with God reinforce the lessons Hagar had learned in her first encounter with Him? How do you think this gave her hope as she and Ishmael began their new life?

God hears our cries and those of our children. God sees us in our troubles, and we are never alone. How can this knowledge give us hope as we and our children face struggles and grief?

Write out Lamentations 3:22-24.

One thing I love about God is the way He patiently corrects and leads me. When I was a younger mom, I was surrounded by drama and struggling through grief. Not a good combination. If you're struggling in one of these areas, I want to gently encourage you to ask the Lord to give you a desire to see any unhealthy relationship patterns or habits you may be engaging in.

Whether it's online or in real life, we all benefit by putting God's relationship rules into practice. But we're not the only ones benefiting, are we? At the end of the day, our kids will benefit most from watching their mom become aware of—and break free from—unnecessary drama. "No-drama mamas" give their families a generational gift when they model right relationships. It's a gift that keeps on giving, and it helps prepare your heart for the times when drama and pain are unavoidable.

The unavoidables are hard, aren't they? Grief and struggle are simply part of the process of becoming. If you're struggling through a loss today, know that God is near. He sees your struggle, and even now He is making a way where there seems to be no way. You can trust Him.

Jesus was acquainted with grief. Over the years, I have taken much comfort in knowing that God understands how I feel when waves of grief knock me off my feet. God is always there to help me stand up again, even though it can feel unbearable. Trust in His heart and His timing for you, sweet mom. Just like He saw Hagar, He sees and loves you. He really is as close as the mention of His name.

Let's Take Action

This week, take some time to write out your thoughts to God. Choose one or more of these journal prompts, or simply allow the Holy Spirit to prompt you as you come before Him in prayer.

Lord, You know that I need to get serious about becoming a no-drama mama and being wise with my words. Please show me a new way to respond in these situations . . .

God, I'm struggling with grief and rejection. Help me to find hope in You, knowing that You hear me and see me and that You are using this pain for something good . . .

Heavenly Father, You are the One who sees me and who hears my cries. You are the One who calls me to a better way to speak and think and live. Please help me as I try to move away from drama and toward Your way of speaking to and about others. You don't promise that my life will be free from pain, but You promise that You are here and that my struggles have a purpose. Teach me to live in that hope. Amen.

Becoming Beautiful

THE ART OF REST

Truly my soul finds rest in God; my salvation comes from him.

— PSALM 62:1, NIV

Charm is deceptive, and beauty does not last;

but a woman who fears the LORD will be greatly praised.

— PROVERBS 31:30

Our study this week focuses on material from chapters 11 and 13 of *Becoming MomStrong*.

Let's Become . . .

MomStrong moms are learning to focus on inner beauty, and they're aware of their need for rest. Definitions of beauty and worth change with the culture, but God says, "Find your worth in Me, and rest."

LET'S START HERE

When do you feel stressed? What activities help you to feel rejuvenated?

What messages does our culture send about bodies and beauty?

LET'S TALK: A Note from Heidi

How much are you carrying this week, my friend? If you're like most moms I know, you're juggling a lot. You're keeping up with schoolwork and doctor appointments . . . and there are bills to pay and dinner to make, and the church needed a new nursery coordinator so you said yes before you had a chance to pray about it. And still, you wonder if you're "doing enough."

Am I close? Today's moms are up against a lot, and I believe the devil is using our stretched-too-thin lifestyles to keep us worn out, weary, and unable to rest.

Here's something I've noticed as I walk through my own motherhood story: tired moms are not battle ready. Tired moms can easily miss important cues from their kids, and they can find themselves unable to enjoy things that would normally bring them joy. I know. I've been that mom on more than one occasion.

Moms who are weary lose perspective, and with this in mind, let's talk about a very real struggle that arises when we don't have God's perspective about our own worth. Most women understand the struggle to make peace with and even—dare I say it—*enjoy* the bodies God gave them. I think we struggle with our self-worth more when we look in the mirror and see a worn-out version of ourselves staring back at us. Maybe it's just me, but I have a hunch you know what I mean.

In a culture that's focused on outward appearance, MomStrong moms challenge each other to be beautiful from the inside out because we know our worth isn't defined by the covers of magazines—and we want our kids to know that too. After all, equipping our kids to navigate the cultural pressures surrounding body image and to find their worth in the way God sees them starts with the way we see ourselves.

If you're struggling to find rest and you long to enjoy the everyday moments that make motherhood so special, keep reading, because God's heart for you is clear: He wants you to learn how to take your weary heart to Him and be refreshed. Then the Spirit of God—the One who raised Jesus from the dead—will live in you (see Romans 8:11).

When the power of Christ rests on you, everything changes. Let's jump in!

— HSJ

Becoming MomStrong

Finding Rest

I start off chapter 11 of *Becoming MomStrong* with a story about an intervention—my own. When my kids came to me and told me I wasn't fun anymore because I was too busy to do what I'd promised and too rushed to enjoy what I *was* doing, I had to stop and reassess my life. I write, "In my effort to make everyone happy, it seemed I wasn't making anyone happy. Including myself. I was struggling to keep up with daily life. I was easily irritated. Things that used to bring me joy no longer did. I needed to hit the reset button."

When we try to do it all, too often we end up falling flat on our faces. We become stressed out and filled with anxiety because we think everything depends on us. But when we take a minute to think straight, we know that's not true, right? The truth is, everything depends on God. Chapter 11 of *Becoming MomStrong* says, "He has a plan, and I promise, it doesn't include burning you out and leaving your family resentful and sad. If we're going to be strong as mothers, we have to start being honest about where we invest our time and energy."

Do you agree that most of the stress we struggle with is self-inflicted? Why or why not?

Do you feel a pull to "do it all"? How do you see this tension play out in your own life?

What kind of stress do you put on yourself? Where do you think the pressure to be a perfect, organized, creative, rock-star mom comes from?

What's on your plate that maybe shouldn't be there? What might be pulling the best of you away from your husband and children?

The truth is, we need rest, and we need it now. We can find refreshment in solitude and hobbies, like crocheting, scrapbooking, reading, journaling, playing a musical instrument, or watching a movie. You might be rejuvenated when you take a long hot bath by yourself or meet a friend at Starbucks. All of those are good things. But MomStrong moms know that we find the truest rest at the feet of Jesus.

Is your tendency to turn to God or something else for rest? Why?

What activities rejuvenate you? How might you be able to fit more of these into your week?

Several passages in Scripture compare our thirst for God to our thirst for water. His presence is as life giving to us as a drink of cool water is to someone walking through the desert. Read the following verses and fill in the blanks below.

Psalm 42:1-2: As the _____ longs for _____ of water, so I long for you, O God. I _____ for God, the living God. When can I go and stand before him?

Psalm 63:1: O God, you are my God; I earnestly _____ for you. My soul _____ for you; my whole body longs for you in this _____ and _____ land where there is no water.

John 7:37-38: Jesus stood and shouted to the crowds, "Anyone who is _____ may come to me! Anyone who believes in me may come and _____! For the Scriptures declare, 'Rivers of _____ will flow from his heart.'"

Why does God's presence refresh us? How have you found time with God to be life giving?

If we know what brings us genuine rest, why don't we seek it out more often? Why do we struggle so much to take time to rest?

Read the statements on the struggle-to-rest test in chapter 11 of *Becoming MomStrong*. Which of these statements sound like you?

In chapter 11, I talk about the three directives Jesus gives in Matthew 11:28-29: "come to me," "take my yoke," and "let me teach you." Let's take a quick look at all three.

> How can we stop wrestling and start resting? We can begin by treating rest as we would any other important commitment or task. (Oh man, am I ever preaching to myself right now!) Ask the Lord for the discipline to turn off any unnecessary distractions. Get alone with God, and then turn your eyes upon Jesus. He promises to give us rest and to refresh us in a way only He can.

Do you struggle to make time to get alone with God and read His Word? If so, why do you think this is?

How can you make coming to God a priority? What changes do you need to make to your schedule to make this happen? Maybe it's getting up earlier, setting a periodic alarm on your phone that reminds you to pray throughout the day, starting a daily Bible reading plan, putting quiet time on your calendar, or asking a friend or your husband to hold you accountable. Write down one thing you will try this week.

In practical terms, what does it mean to take up the yoke of Christ? It means listening to God for direction. When we take His yoke, we're taking only the assignments He gives us. Nothing more, nothing less. His yoke, His timing.

What commitments do you have right now that might not be God's best for you? What is encouraging about this concept of sharing a yoke with God?

In order to learn from Jesus, we have to be in His Word. Learning from Jesus requires prayer and quiet reflection. . . . Becoming MomStrong means that we become students of the Lord. Mothers are also teachers, and when a mom learns from the Lord, so do her children. It sounds easier than it is, I know—especially in times of stress and struggle. Most of us aren't born with the ability to just chill out in the middle of stress. We need to learn.

How can we learn to wait quietly before God? How do times of quiet reflection and prayer help us to focus on how God wants us to live?

Take a few minutes right now to sit quietly before God. Meditate on a passage of Scripture or an attribute of God. When your thoughts wander, bring them back to Him. Rest in His presence.

True Beauty

I bet you can remember moments that shaped your ideas about what was beautiful, how you felt about your body, and who got to decide if you were worthwhile. Maybe it was an interaction between your parents, like in my story at the beginning of chapter 13. Maybe it was a neighbor kid who laughed at your clothes or a junior high boy who made it clear that he didn't consider you one of the pretty girls in the class. Or maybe it was magazine covers that highlighted only one version of beauty, leaving you to conclude that any other look just didn't measure up.

What messages about beauty and body image did you pick up in childhood or adolescence? How do those messages still affect you today?

As we consider how to pass on a godly perspective on beauty and sexuality to our children, we need to start with what God says. As chapter 13 of *Becoming MomStrong* says, "MomStrong moms know that they are created in the image of God and that God doesn't create anything that is less than wonderful."

Write Psalm 139:14 below.

Look up Ephesians 2:10 and fill in the blanks.

We are God's _____. He has created us _____ in Christ Jesus, so we can do the good things he _____ for us long ago.

What do you think it means to be God's masterpiece? What's one way you can help your children understand their immense value to God?

Our culture defines worth based on external beauty. But we know better. Chapter 13 of *Becoming MomStrong* says,

> MomStrong moms know that while the world focuses on the outside, God's gaze is focused on the inner woman. That doesn't mean we shouldn't take good care of ourselves. . . . God wants us all to remember that our true worth and beauty come from being daughters of the King of kings.

What pressure do you feel to look a certain way? How might knowing you are valuable as a child of God help to relieve some of this pressure?

What does it mean for your body to be a temple of the Holy Spirit (see 1 Corinthians 6:19)? How should this affect the way you think about your appearance?

Not only is our culture obsessed with beauty, but it's also terrified of growing older. Take one trip down the beauty aisle at your local drugstore, and you'll see that the shelves are overflowing with "anti-aging" products. Plastic surgeons and pharmaceutical companies promise to keep us young, but we all know the truth: we can't hold back time. Our bodies and faces won't look the same as they did ten or twenty years ago—and that's okay, because that's not our ultimate goal.

Read the following verses on beauty and fill in the blanks below.

1 Peter 3:3-4: Don't be concerned about the _____ beauty of fancy _____, expensive _____, or beautiful _____. You should clothe yourselves instead with the beauty that comes from _____, the _____ beauty of a _____ and _____ spirit, which is so precious to God.

Proverbs 31:30: Charm is _____, and beauty does not _____; but a woman who _____ the Lord will be greatly praised.

What happens when we make outer beauty our focus?

Why doesn't inner beauty fade? Why does God value a gentle and quiet spirit?

While we're on this topic, we need to take a minute to talk about sex and marriage. All too often, we women let our frustrations with our own bodies get in the way of our sexual relationship with our husbands. We're assuming they expect us to look a certain way—but most often, they don't! Chapter 13 of *Becoming MomStrong* says, "God's original intent was that a husband and a wife would be one flesh—without the shame and embarrassment the world has put on us."

Have you noticed how the way you view your body can affect sex with your husband? How would your interaction with your husband change if you were more confident in your own skin, flaws and all?

As we teach our children about beauty, their bodies, and God's design for sex, we have important lessons to offer both our sons and our daughters.

In what ways does our culture have low expectations for men? How can we raise these expectations for our own sons?

I want my children to see themselves through God's lens, not the lens of the world.

With so much confusion about the role of the sexes in our world today, it's not surprising that many parents struggle to teach their boys how to embrace their own masculinity. Has the culture's vilification of masculinity affected the way you parent your son? If so, how?

Write out Micah 6:8.

With this verse in mind, what is the most important thing we can teach our sons about God's true design for masculinity?

In the Garden of Eden, the man was commissioned to do two things. Read Genesis 2:15 and write down both tasks.

Are you teaching your sons to work? To treat women with respect and kindness? How are you and your husband modeling this in your marriage?

As moms, the way we think about ourselves will have a direct impact on the way our girls view themselves. The first thing they need to know from you is something you need to let sink down deep into your heart: *you are deeply loved by God*.

When you think of your daughter growing into a woman who is healthy and whole, what do you see?

Think over the past week. What are some ways you have modeled a sense of worth for your daughters?

Read Genesis 2:21-22. The Bible teaches that women were created to be helpers. In today's supercharged discussions, it's more important than ever that God's daughters understand what this means. The Hebrew for *helper* is *ezer*, and it doesn't imply someone who is "less than." In fact, the word *ezer* is a powerful one and is used most often in the Bible in reference to the Lord being our helper.

Write out Psalm 33:20.

The Lord is our helper, enriching our lives and helping us be more fruitful than we would be without His help. Can you imagine? God created you—and your daughters—to fill this very special need, whether married or not. In all of creation, women are seen as bringing life, beauty, and strength into this world according to God's wonderful plan.

Throughout Scripture, women who walk with God are commended for being brave and courageous, as we studied in week one.

List at least one godly character trait demonstrated by each of these amazing women.

Judges 4 (Deborah)

Joshua 2, 6 (Rahab)

Ruth 1 (Ruth)

Luke 1:26-56 (Mary, the mother of Jesus)

A Voice from the Bible: Mary

This week we'll be spending time with a woman best known for something she didn't do. Mary, the sister of Martha and Lazarus, was a woman of great inner beauty who knew how to find rest in God.

As Jesus and His disciples were traveling to Jerusalem, they passed through the small town of Bethany. Martha invited them into her home—perhaps just for a meal or perhaps to stay overnight. Either way, it was a big group, and most of us know that feeding a whole lot of people is a whole lot of work. Martha did what most of us would do and jumped into high-efficiency mode—preparing food, cleaning, arranging the table just so. But Mary?

Read Luke 10:39 and fill in the blanks below.

Her sister, Mary, sat at the Lord's _____, _____ to what he taught.

If you can identify with Martha, like I can, you might be tempted to paint Mary as a little irresponsible. She must have been the baby of the family, right? The one who never noticed what needed to be done and just assumed someone else would do all the work? Well, maybe. But Scripture doesn't really show us an irresponsible person so much as a mesmerized one. In a room full of men, Mary crept close to Jesus so she could hear His teaching. We can imagine her hanging on His every word.

Martha found herself alone in the kitchen, and she couldn't take it. Read her response in Luke 10:40 and fill in the blanks below.

Martha was distracted by the big _____ she was preparing. She came to Jesus and said, "Lord, doesn't it seem _____ to you that my sister just sits here while I do all the _____? Tell her to come and _____ me."

How do you respond to people who aren't caught up in your busyness or who don't share your priorities?

Have you ever noticed that when we're busy, we want others to be busy? If I'm running around the house trying to eradicate every speck of dust and get rid of the piles of clutter on the counter, I might look at my husband reading his Bible on the couch and think, *He's lazy. Why isn't he helping me?* The truth is, looking down at him might even make me feel a little bit better about myself and my own productivity. It wouldn't even occur to me that his priorities might be right and mine might be wrong. That's exactly where Martha was. But then Jesus gently set her straight.

Write out Luke 10:41-42 below.

What is the one thing worth being concerned about? Why won't it be taken away from Mary?

Many of us wouldn't be too happy to be told that we were too upset over details when the "details" involved feeding more than a dozen people on our watch. Am I right? But I like to think that Martha was able to understand Jesus' words and the heart behind them. He knew people needed to eat; I don't think He was telling her that her cooking was unimportant. Her problem was thinking that the details of her hospitality were more important than anything else.

What things do you tend to think of as more important than spending time with God?

I wonder if Martha sat down and listened to Jesus for a while, focusing on who He was and what He was teaching. And then maybe when she went back to the kitchen to finish the food, her attitude was different. She still cared about the food—don't get me wrong—but she realized that her number one goal wasn't to win the disciples' vote for "best cook" but to simply spend time with Jesus.

Whenever I read the story of Mary and Martha, I always cringe a little . . . because, as I'm sure you've guessed, I'm naturally more of a Martha than a Mary. I like my lists. I crave productivity and enjoy seeing the fruit of hard work. Those things aren't bad in and of themselves, but when they rob us of time with our Savior, we end up weaker, no matter how many things we've checked off our list that day or that week.

As we end this week, ask the Lord, "Am I spending my time in a way that pleases You?" That simple question is a key that can unlock all kinds of fears and insecurities, including, *Where will I find the time to spend with God? What if God wants me to give something up so I can become the wife and mother He wants me to be?*

Jesus wants moms today to take His yoke and carry His burden—not someone else's. This looks different for each of us, but one thing remains the same: when we yield to God's still, small voice, the impossible becomes possible, and rest is always the result.

Let's Take Action

This week, take some time to write out your thoughts to God. Choose one or more of the following journal prompts:

God, I want to start each day with You. Help me to come to You each morning and ask for guidance. Today I need . . .

I can get hung up on my appearance, spending too much time trying to buy the right clothes, get the right hairstyle, and compete with the women around me. But I'm exhausted, Lord. I want to figure out what true beauty means . . .

Lord God, spending time with You offers so much—rest, rejuvenation, a realigned mind-set. Forgive me for not making these things priorities. Please help me to come to You, take Your yoke, and learn from You— because you have promised to give me rest. When I'm too focused on my outward appearance, remind me that Your true beauty will never fade. Please help me to care more about my heart than about physical beauty, both in myself and in my children. Amen.

Becoming Unshakable

THE ART OF WALKING IN GRACE AND TRUTH

As iron sharpens iron, so a friend sharpens a friend.

⌐ PROVERBS 27:17

The grass withers and the flowers fade,

but the word of our God stands forever.

⌐ ISAIAH 40:8

Let's Become . . .

MomStrong moms are becoming absolutely aware of the truth of God's Word. They're committed to knowing God's Word as they grow in genuine community.

LET'S START HERE

Who are your closest mom friends? What do you find most encouraging about those relationships?

In what situations do you feel you can rely on God's Word? What parts of Scripture do you sometimes question?

LET'S TALK: *A Note from Heidi*

Friendship is such a precious gift, isn't it? Friends can help us see through the lies we accidentally let through our truth filter, because true friends tell the truth—even when we don't want to hear it. A good friend isn't bothered by the fact that you forgot her birthday or missed a text message; she sees the best in you. She knows your love language, and you know hers; and every once in a while, you sit back and smile at the thought of her. I've been privileged to have just a few of these lifelong friends over the years, and this week, we're going to spend some time talking about building a sisterhood that will see you through each season of your life.

MomStrong moms cheer each other on—so let's get started!

— H&J

Becoming MomStrong

Finding Community

We all need some mom friends—women who are in our stage of life (or who used to be) and who understand what it's like to walk a colicky baby around the living room for hours, to be so tired you can't remember your children's names, and to be so proud of those same children that your heart nearly bursts. We need a community of women who will encourage us, build us up, cry and laugh with us, and continually point us back to Christ.

It can be a struggle to build this kind of community. Being a mother, especially of young children, can be isolating. In chapter 14 of *Becoming MomStrong*, I write,

> Isolation contributes to depression, anger, and sadness by feeding on our fears about our worth and purpose. That's why the devil works so hard to keep mothers feeling isolated and alone: he knows that if moms are distracted from their mission, their children are much easier targets. . . . Moms need other moms. Building strong friendships is foundational to becoming MomStrong.

Read Ecclesiastes 4:9-10 and fill in the blanks below.

Two people are _____ off than one, for they can help each other _____. If one person falls, the other can reach out and _____. But someone who falls _____ is in real trouble.

How can genuine, godly friends support each other? What is one tangible way a friend has helped you in the past or you have helped a friend?

If you're struggling to make friends, ask God to help you make connections. Think about places where you might meet moms—a moms' group at church, story time at the library, a mom-and-me gymnastics class, or a neighborhood play date. Look around for other women who might be isolated. How can you start to build a community?

I write a blog and run an online community, so I appreciate the value of online relationships. Yet online friends can't babysit your kids at ten minutes' notice because you have to take one child to the ER to get stitches. Online friends can't drop off a meal when you have a family emergency. Chapter 14 of *Becoming MomStrong* says, "There's no substitute for walking in relationship with moms who actually show up and do life with you as opposed to just casually commenting about it. . . . We're designed to be connected with other people."

Look up the following verses. What does each tell us about how relationships can encourage us in our faith and in our daily lives?

Proverbs 27:17

Hebrews 10:24-25

Proverbs 17:17

Write out Matthew 6:33.

Perfectionism is one of the biggest enemies of genuine community. In this passage from Matthew, Jesus clearly tells us that He wants us to seek Him before anything else. It's not wrong to work at things we enjoy or to set high goals for ourselves; the problem comes when those things become our primary focus. Jesus is saying, "Make Me your *first* priority!"

Do your friends encourage you to make your relationship with God a priority in your life?

What are some ways we can sharpen each other in this area?

The Internet has made it easy to hide our reality. When we're online, we can present only our best side and never show our weak spots. As chapter 14 of *Becoming MomStrong* puts it, "We think everyone else has it all together, so we shy away from showing them who we truly are. . . . This pursuit of perfection consumes our time and exhausts us—and Satan knows that."

Write out 1 Corinthians 11:1.

Who do you tend to compare yourself to? In what ways has perfectionism kept you from reaching out to others or focusing on what really matters?

The irony is that our desire to look perfect often keeps us from developing strong friendships. Here's something I've observed in my own pursuit of true community: nothing brings people together like a good, honest failure. Chapter 14 of *Becoming MomStrong* says, "We don't identify with Pinterest-perfect DIY projects and perfectly posed family portraits. We identify with the mess. No one is encouraged by a mom who pretends to have it all together, because everyone knows it's not true."

Think of a relationship you have in real life where you bonded over a shared struggle. Why does sharing our mistakes with others draw us closer to them? How can sharing these mistakes help us point each other to God?

One of the benefits of living in community is the accountability it brings—not only to us, but to our children, who can have a whole community of mothers. (Lucky them!) I tell a story about my own community of moms—my sisterhood of spies—in chapter 14 of *Becoming MomStrong*: "There is power in living in community with other moms. I want to encourage you to get to know the mothers of the children your kids hang out with. Let them know you're looking to form a sisterhood. Keep an eye out for their kids, and I promise they'll return the favor."

How have your children grown because of their relationships with your friends or other trusted adults? How can you look out for other children in your community?

Trusting in the Authority of Scripture

Write out John 10:27.

The term *sola Scriptura*, or "the Bible alone," is a short phrase that reminds us of a simple truth: for Christians, the Bible is the final authority on all matters of faith and morality. As we reach the end of this six-week journey, we get to the most important quality of MomStrong moms: an unshakable trust in the authority of Scripture. We need this resolute faith because raising the children God has given to us is the most important job we'll ever have.

In chapter 15 of *Becoming MomStrong* I write,

> Think about it: God trusts us to raise His children. They're not really ours, after all. They're on loan to us from the Creator. Our job is to train these precious children to hear God's still, small voice above all the other voices competing for their attention—both today and in the years to come.

How does it change your perspective on parenting to realize that your children belong to God?

Write out 2 Timothy 3:16-17.

What point is the apostle Paul making about the importance of knowing God's Word?

What are some questions your children are asking about who God is or what it means to live a Christian life?

Read Psalm 119:160. What will help you answer your children effectively when they ask you about following the Lord?

When we have questions about what to do and how to live, the Holy Spirit guides us. We can also receive wise counsel from friends, family members, and other believers. But the number one way we receive God's truth is through the words of Scripture—His words. Chapter 15 of *Becoming MomStrong* says, "The God-breathed, unchanging, inerrant, comprehensive, life-giving Word of God is our only source of truth! The moment we decide that we can cherry-pick which parts of the Bible are true and which parts are not, the battle is lost."

Write out 2 Peter 1:20-21.

What claim does the Bible make about its origin and inspiration?

How can we increase our trust in the Bible?

There is power in living in community with other moms.

Write out Isaiah 40:8 below. What does it remind us about God's Word?

Every year our culture moves farther from the way God wants us to live. We can't trust what society says about God—and sometimes we can't even trust our own judgment. We must rely on God. Chapter 15 of *Becoming MomStrong* says, "Our children need to know what God actually says, not what our culture wants Him to say. MomStrong moms understand the difference, and they point their children back to the authority of Scripture."

What is one area you've noticed where the world's definition of right and wrong is different from God's?

Look up Romans 16:17. Why do you think Paul uses such strong words in this warning?

What happens when we trust people's wisdom instead of God's?

There are no shortcuts to knowing God's Word. The only way we can let Scripture sink into our hearts is to study it for ourselves. We need to take responsibility for our own faith by prayerfully studying the Word and getting serious about our own walk with God.

What proactive steps can you take to get serious about your walk with God?

Psalm 119:11 talks about hiding God's Word in our hearts. Write out this verse below.

What can you do this week to hide God's Word in your heart and in the hearts of your children? Here are a few ideas: (1) text yourself Scripture; (2) sign up for my daily Scripture writing challenge (it includes copy work and lined paper for your children!) at www.heidistjohn.com/scripturewriting; (3) write out Bible verses and post them around your house; (4) listen to an audio recording of Scripture in the car or while you work around the house; (5) find Scripture set to music and play it during the day.

Being in God's Word every day helps us stand firm, even as the sands of culture shift under our feet.

The apostle Paul warns that one day people won't receive wise teaching but will listen only to what they want to hear. Look up 2 Timothy 4:3 and fill in the blanks below.

A time is coming when people will no longer listen to _____ and _____ teaching. They will follow their own _____ and will look for teachers who will tell them whatever their _____ ears want to hear.

The day Paul described is now. MomStrong moms choose to believe God over culture, as *Becoming MomStrong* says in chapter 15: "When we realize the truth of Paul's warning, there are two reactions that can drive us: one is fear, and the other is faith."

What can give us confidence even when we realize that the world around us is moving further from God?

Look up Psalm 1:1-3. How do these verses describe those who study God's Word? Why are these people so firmly rooted?

The Bible gives us answers to questions we face today, but it's so much more than just a book of morals. Chapter 15 of *Becoming MomStrong* says,

> God's heart for people is all over the Bible. Throughout the pages of Scripture, broken people find the truth that makes them whole, lost people are found, and those who are trapped in cycles of shame are set free.

This is life-giving stuff! We need to hear it every day to make sense of our lives, and our children need to hear it too.

When has the Bible brought you joy and comfort?

Do you have a favorite verse that challenges or encourages you? Write it here.

Let's end with the most important thing (from chapter 15 of *Becoming MomStrong*):

> If we're going to call ourselves Christians, our lives need
> to bring God glory. My prayer is that God will raise up a
> generation of parents whose sole goal is to teach and equip
> their children to be strong in the Lord and to hear His voice
> by the way they live their lives.

How can you strive to bring God glory through your parenting?

What could help you teach and equip your children to be strong in the Lord and to hear His voice? Write down a few ideas here.

MomStrong
moms let the
Creator define
the truth.

A Voice from the Bible: Priscilla

In this last week of our study, we're going to look at a lesser-known woman from the New Testament. She is mentioned just seven times, yet we can tell she was firmly grounded in the Word of God.

We first meet Priscilla (or Prisca, as she's sometimes called) in Acts 18:1-3. Read the passage below and fill in the blanks.

Paul left Athens and went to _____. There he became acquainted with a Jew named _____, born in Pontus, who had recently arrived from Italy with his wife, _____. They had left Italy when Claudius Caesar _____ all Jews from Rome. Paul lived and worked with them, for they were _____ just as he was.

The passage doesn't tell us much about Priscilla, but we know that Aquila was a Jew born in a region close to modern-day Turkey. We also know that he and Priscilla ended up in Italy but later had to leave—probably abruptly—because of the emperor's orders. They were starting over in a new place.

It's no coincidence that their paths crossed with Paul's. If you've ever moved to a new city, you know that one of the first things you do is start looking for your people. You need to begin building a new community, and as Jews, Priscilla and Aquila would have done that at the synagogue. That's probably where they met Paul.

How have you found support from a community of people who share your faith? How might your community of believers reach out to someone who is new?

It's likely that Priscilla and Aquila were already Christians when they arrived in Corinth. As they lived and worked with Paul, they no doubt heard the story of his dramatic conversion, talked about the Scriptures that prophesied the coming Messiah, and discussed what it meant to be saved by faith. Maybe they even got to preview a few of Paul's epistles before he sent them! I have no doubt they were in the Word together every day.

Acts 18:4-17 records some of Paul's ministry work in Corinth. Write out verse 11 below.

Paul was busy with ministry, and it's likely that Priscilla and Aquila were involved in serving too. Eventually, when Paul traveled to Ephesus, they joined him there. When Paul left for a longer journey, they stayed behind in Ephesus, where they continued to play a significant role in developing and strengthening the church.

Read Acts 18:24-26 and fill in the blanks below.

A Jew named _____, an eloquent speaker who knew the Scriptures well, had arrived in Ephesus from Alexandria in Egypt. He had been taught the way of the Lord, and he taught others about _____ with an _____ spirit and with accuracy. However, he knew only about _____ baptism. When Priscilla and Aquila heard him preaching boldly in the synagogue, they took him aside and _____ the way of God even more _____.

Apollos, the new guy in town, was a bold preacher who sounded like he knew what he was talking about. But Priscilla and Aquila could tell that some of his teachings weren't quite right. When the Bible says Apollos "knew only about John's baptism," that probably meant he hadn't heard about the instructions Jesus gave before He returned to heaven.

Read Matthew 28:18-20. Who does Jesus say should be baptized?

Apollos clearly knew some things about Jesus. However, if Apollos hadn't heard about the Great Commission, some scholars believe he might not have even heard of Jesus' resurrection. He probably didn't know about Jesus' full work of salvation.

The bottom line? He was preaching an incomplete gospel.

How did Priscilla and Aquila know that what Apollos was teaching wasn't accurate? How did they go about correcting him?

Read Acts 18:27-28. What did Apollos do after he left Ephesus?

Priscilla and Aquila's careful teaching of Apollos had eternal conse-quences. Apollos clearly excelled at speaking and debating, and his work was beneficial for the church. But before he could teach the right things, he needed to know the right things. Priscilla and Aquila were able to teach him because their time studying the Scriptures and working with Paul had given them a rock-solid understanding of the gospel.

You may be wondering why this story seems to be as much about Aquila as it is about Priscilla. In Scripture they are always mentioned together—and that's highly unusual given that they lived in a culture where women didn't have much status or, in many cases, much education. The fact that Priscilla's name comes up every time Aquila is mentioned shows that she was actively involved in ministry and teaching.

Paul mentions Priscilla and Aquila three times in his epistles. Look up Romans 16:3. How does Paul describe this couple?

It's hard to think of much higher praise than being called Paul's coworker in the ministry of Christ. And yet that's what happened to this woman who was solidly grounded in the Word. And we, too, can be part of this wonderful ministry of Christ as we immerse ourselves in Scrip-ture and share it with others.

LET'S REVIEW

I had a singular goal in writing *Becoming MomStrong*: to point women to the Word of God. The Bible is as relevant now as it was when it was written—and I think we could argue that it's needed more than ever before. Oh, how our children need to see their parents "strong in the Lord and in his mighty power" (Ephesians 6:10).

Motherhood is missional in nature, and for followers of Jesus, the mission is clear: to raise our kids to follow Him. The Bible tells us that we have an active adversary, the devil, and that the only way to be on guard against him is to know God and apply His Word to our lives every day. When we know His Word, we know His heart. God's heart is that no one would perish (see 2 Peter 3:9), and that knowledge should propel every Christian to grow in grace and truth. That's what becoming MomStrong is all about.

Of course, we need to grow ourselves before we can pass truth on to our children. We can't give them what we don't have, so let's commit to going all in to follow Jesus. Will you continue the journey with me? While we can't guarantee that our children will come to faith in Christ, we can give them a drink of cool living water from the Word every day and encourage them toward the truth.

Becoming MomStrong means prioritizing your family according to God's wonderful plan. When you do that, beautiful things happen—the kinds of things that moms who love Jesus pray for. Becoming MomStrong means committing to be the mom God created you to be—a worker who doesn't need to be ashamed and who can correctly explain the Word of God (see 2 Timothy 2:15). Becoming MomStrong means praying for our children and nurturing our marriages.

In short, becoming MomStrong means committing to following Jesus.

This generation of moms is shepherding a very special generation of children, and it's my prayer that we would look into the faces of the children God has entrusted to our care and be the hands and feet of Jesus to them. To be MomStrong is generational in scope. In just a few short years, you'll be looking into the faces of your grandchildren, and the prayer will continue: *Lord, teach me so I can point my children and my grandchildren to walk in Your wonderful love.*

Mom, the role you play in the lives of your children can't be measured by earthly standards, because what you're doing carries with it eternal significance. Every ounce of energy, sacrifice, and prayer you pour into your family is worth it. When you place your confidence in an unchanging God, your confidence is well placed. After all, He is the source of true strength.

Let's Take Action

This week, take some time to write out your thoughts to God. Choose one or more of the following journal prompts:

I need a strong community of mom friends around me, but sometimes I feel alone. Please help me to develop good friends—those who will . . .

I want to be strong in my faith, and I know that means I need to know Your Word better. Here's what I want to do to make that happen . . .

Dear Lord, please show me how to strengthen the community around me. I need friends, and I want to be a good friend too—the kind who points others back to You. I know that You alone are my rock, and the only way I will stand firm in You is to know what You have told me through Your Word. Help me to commit to studying the Bible and trusting its authority. I know this will help me and my children as we seek to develop an unshakable faith. Amen.

About the Author

Heidi St. John is a popular conference speaker, author, and blogger at *The Busy Mom*. Heidi speaks all over the country sharing encouraging, relevant, biblical truth with women. Heidi and her husband, Jay, are the founders and executive directors of Firmly Planted Family, an organization focused on family discipleship. The St. Johns live in Washington State, where they enjoy life with their seven children. When Heidi isn't homeschooling, babysitting her grandchildren, writing, traveling, or speaking, she can be found with her husband enjoying a cup of coffee and the view from their home in the Pacific Northwest.

BECOMING MOM STRONG

HeidiStJohn.com